CONTEMPORARY TANGOS, SAMBAS AND LATIN BALLADS FOR GUITAR

MICHAEL N. BELLMONT

To access the online audio go to:
WWW.MELBAY.COM/30587MEB

© 2020 by Mel Bay Publications, Inc. All Rights Reserved.

WWW.MELBAY.COM

Dedication and Musings

With humility and gratitude my deepest thanks go to William Bay for publishing the compositions herein. "Tango para Guillermo" *(Tango for William)* was specially written for and dedicated to him.

This collection would not exist but for the persistent and steadfast encouragement of two individuals: my wife, Alice; and my long-time friend, Steve Armstrong, a superb guitarist and musician who was an invaluable consultant in the compositional process.

I dedicate this work to the many ordinary folks in countless communities who toil ardently to express themselves through some art or craft, producing work worthy of a world stage while remaining largely unknown.

In 1978 I completed a Bachelor of Music degree in Classical Guitar performance. However, I chose to put aside my dream of becoming a professional musician and joined my father's insurance business to support my young family. Thus, I assigned the nurture and honing of my musical skills to late nights after putting the kids to bed and the household was fast asleep.

That decision placed me in the company of some well-known composers in history whose primary professions were other than in music, including the innovative and imaginative American composer, Charles Ives who was an insurance agent; the great naval officer/composer Nikolai Rimsky-Korsakov; and Alexander Borodin, a renowned chemist.

It is tempting to conjure up a mystique around creating and composing, portraying them as some special magic with which one has been endowed. However, the simple truth is that composing, at its root, is just *makin' stuff up*. That said, as with any worthy endeavor, practice and persistence must be constant companions, not to mention the usefulness of studying music formally! Put another way, "*I was obliged to be industrious. Whoever is equally industrious will succeed equally well*" (J. S. Bach). From yet another notable composer, "*It is a mistake to think that the practice of my art has become easy to me. I assure you….no one has given so much care to the study of composition as I.*" (W. A. Mozart).

Composing feels less to me like a gift and more like being a "musical archeologist," dusting off and uncovering tunes that seem to have always been there, buried beneath layers of earth. I simply stumble upon them, discovering a fragment of a melody here and an interesting chord progression there. Each time, after completing the assembly of shards and bones, I wonder how it all happened and whether I will have the good fortune to be included in yet another dig. Remarkably, an idea inevitably follows, or more accurately, I follow another idea!

Here, for your enjoyment, are a few of those shards and bones - assembled, fleshed out, and performed to the best of my abilities.

Musically Yours,

Contents

Title	Page	Audio
Ghost Lover	5	1
Dance of the Goblins	8	2
Island Dream	14	3
Make Believe	17	4
Nocturne	20	5
Pajarito	23	6
Passage	26	7
Rain/After the Rain	29	8
Something Samba	32	9
Soñadora	36	10
Sueño Español	39	11
Tango Cromático	42	12
Tango Español	46	13
Tango Loco	49	14
Tango para Guillermo	54	15
Texas Tango	58	16

Thoughts, Tips, and Technical Terms

"Hinge"

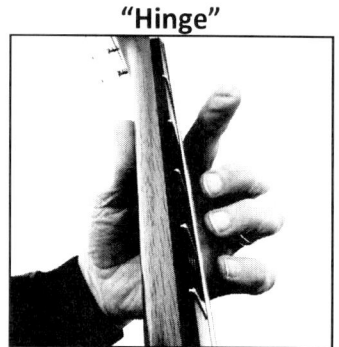

Fret the first string with the base of the first finger.

"Cross fret & Hinge"

Fret the first string with the base of the first finger while reaching across to the next fret for the bass note.

Here are a few thoughts that may be helpful:

- Some of the pieces in this collection vary slightly from the accompanying recordings. Most of the compositions were performed and recorded prior to being committed to notation during which process I occasionally made minor changes.
- With a few exceptions I have chosen to leave out right-hand fingerings as there are so many possible variations. Players that have the technical ability to tackle these pieces are certainly capable of applying their own fingerings.
- The abundant left-hand fingerings are not set in stone, so feel free to depart from them if you find others that are more effective or natural to you. There are a few passages that offer alternative fingerings which appear in parentheses.
- The modified steel-string Gallagher guitar used in the recordings has a wide fretboard which is 2 1/8" at the nut, thus affording the feel of a classical guitar.
- Though all of the compositions in this collection can be readily performed on a nylon-string classical guitar with excellent effect, I chose the steel-string primarily for its ability to sustain the legato melodies. After all, the great classical guitarist/composer of the early 20th Century, Agustín Barrios Mangoré, is believed to have used steel strings.

Since many of the selections evoke improvisational styles that reflect an organic, at times ethnic ethos, you are welcome to give them your own "*accent*" while retaining the integrity of the composition.

Above all, elevate passion over perfection when performing these works. Certainly enough correct notes and proper technique are critical to bringing any opus to life...but let the spirit of Beethoven guide you by adhering to his wise words, *"To play a wrong note is insignificant; to play without passion is inexcusable."*

If you would like to contact me (i.e. to share which piece from the collection is your favorite, send a link to your performance of one of the compositions, or just to "talk shop") my email is michaelbellmont@yahoo.com.

Ghost Lover

Michael N. Bellmont

Dance of the Goblins
(a tango)

Michael N. Bellmont

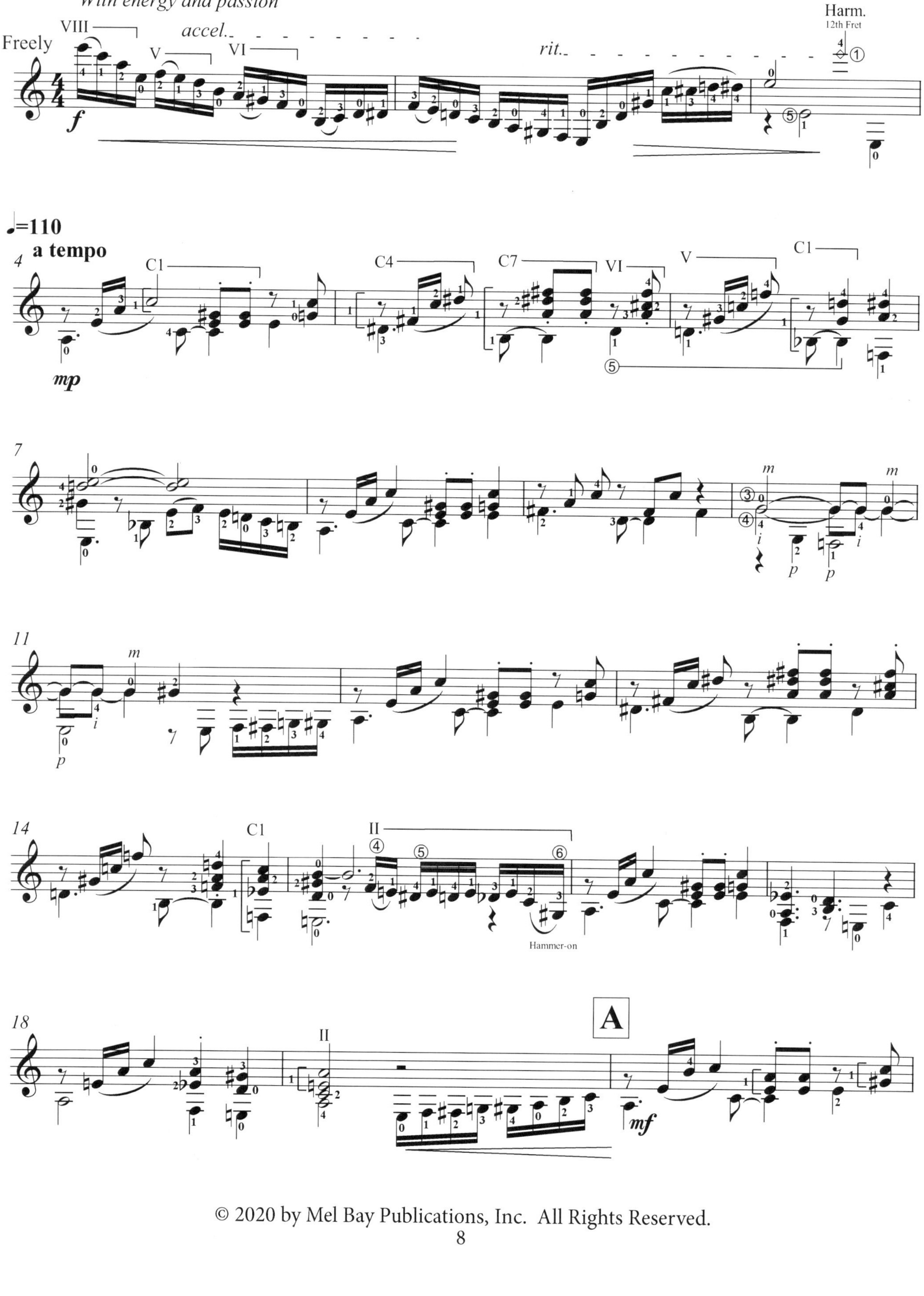

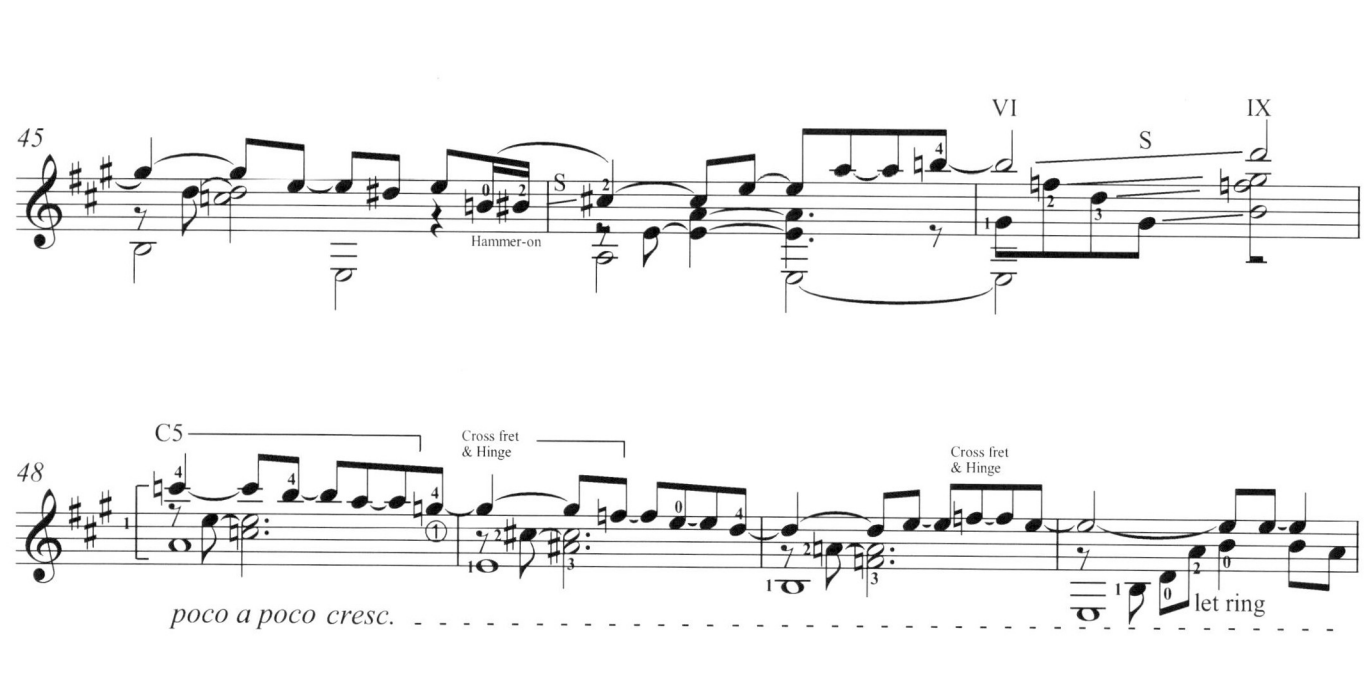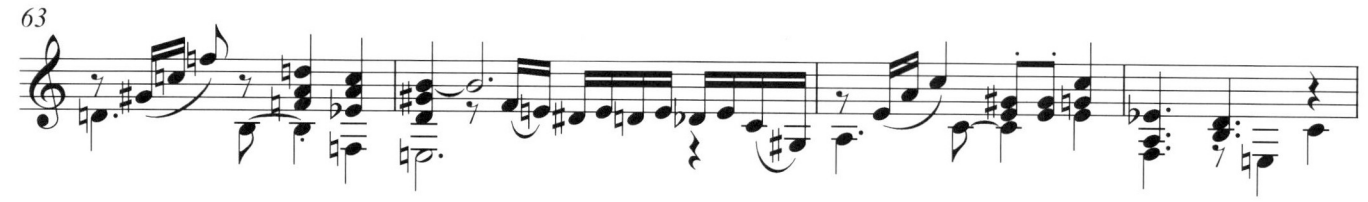

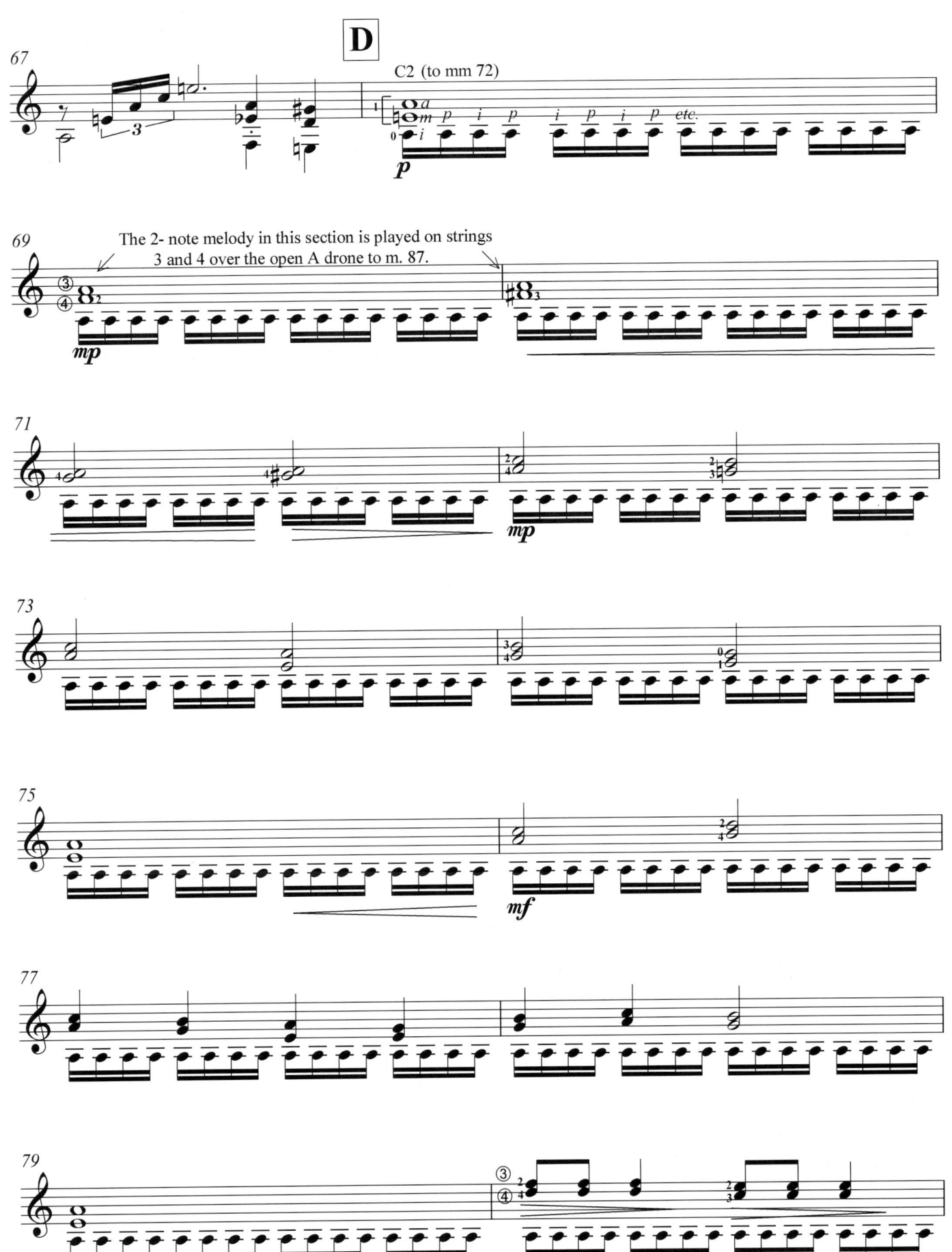

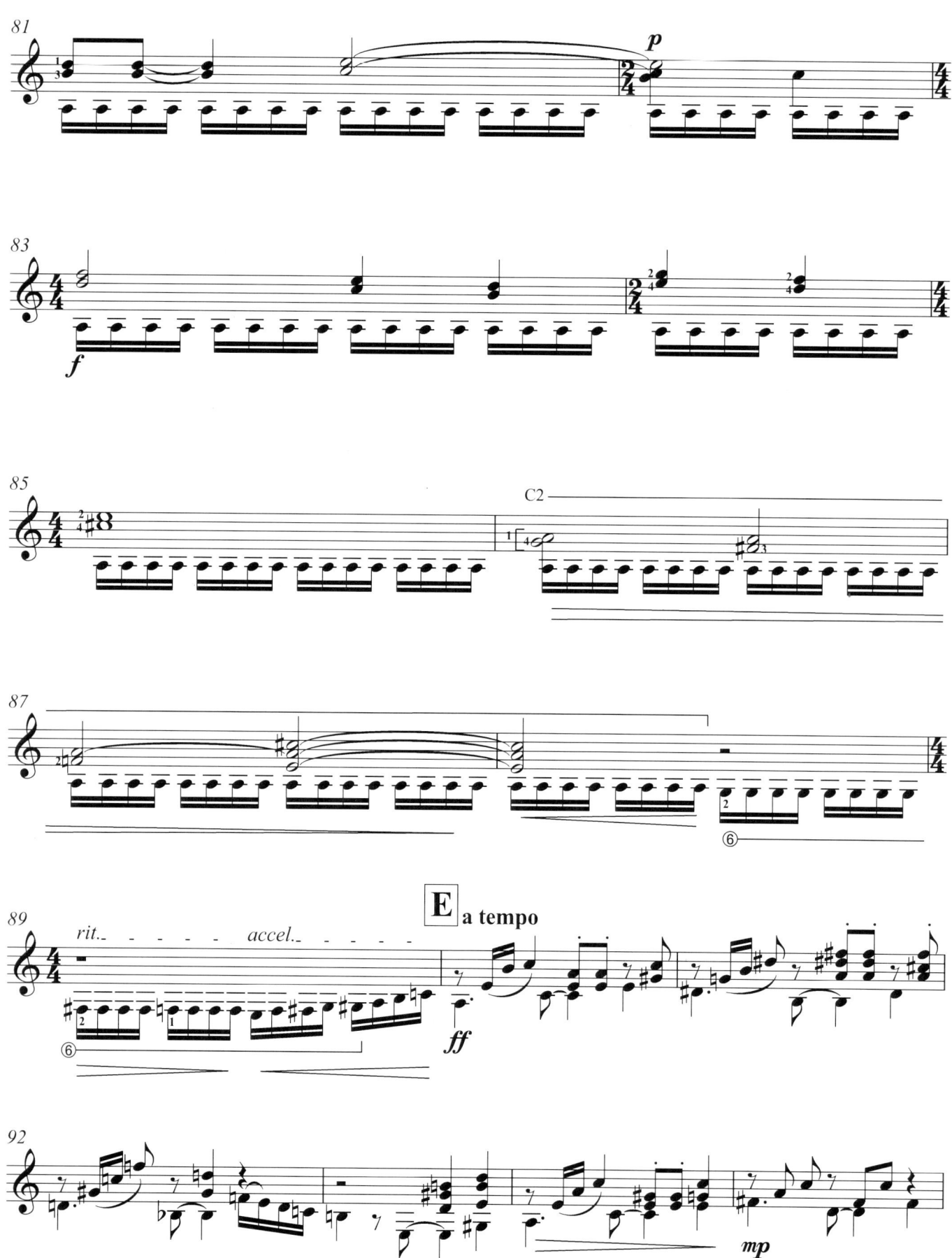

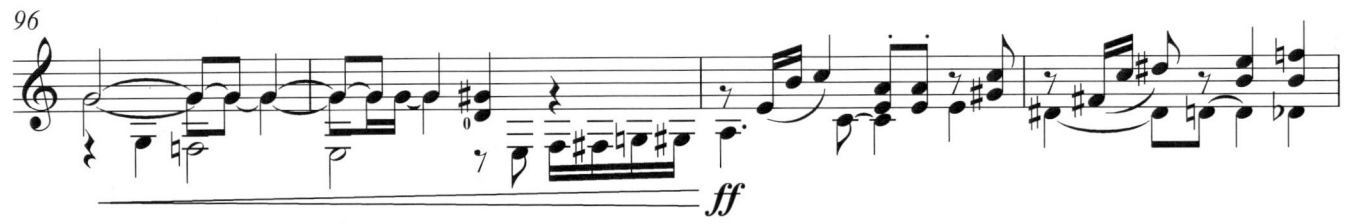

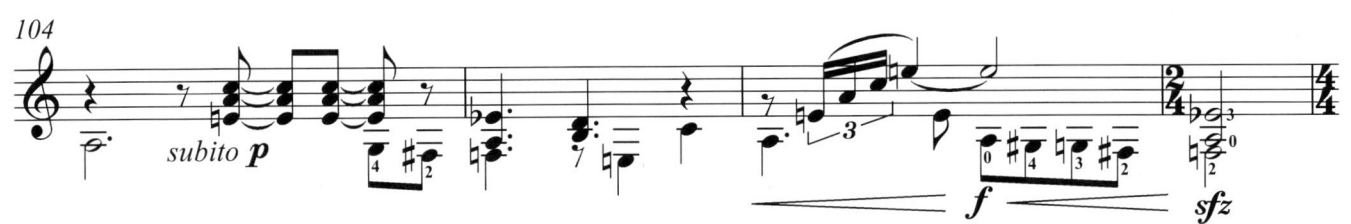
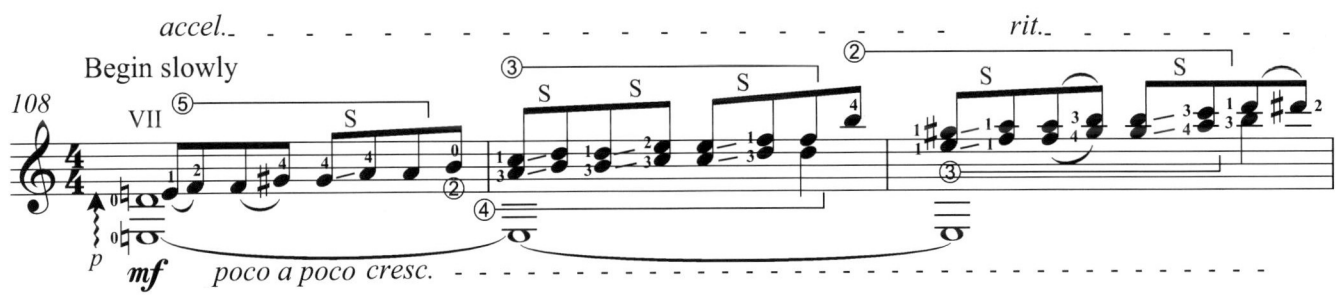
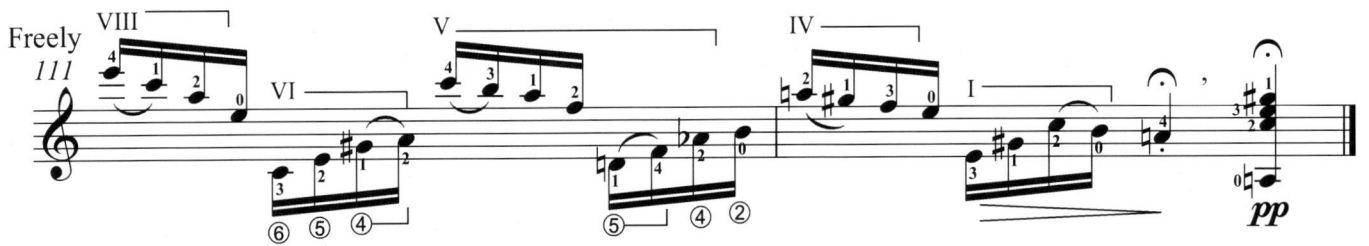

Island Dream

♩=54 S = Slide
⑥ = D
With a relaxed feel
C2

Michael N. Bellmont

pizz. in bass
(To m. 12)

end pizz.

Make Believe

Michael N. Bellmont

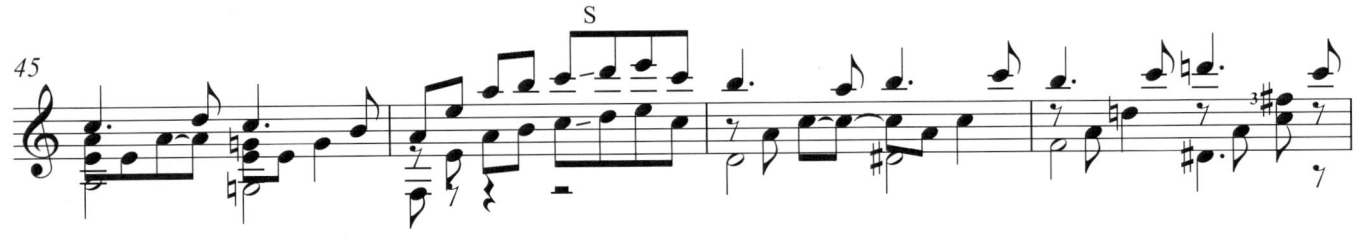
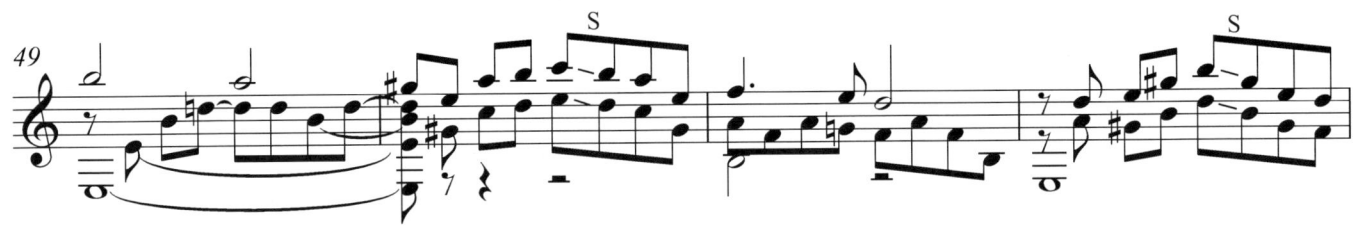
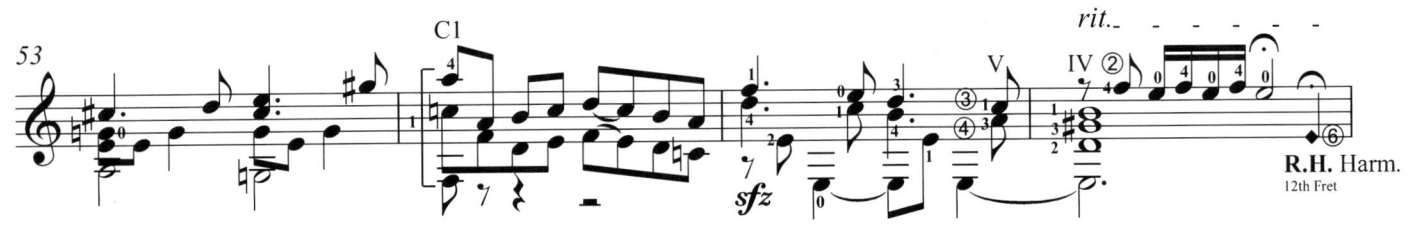

Nocturne

Michael N. Bellmont

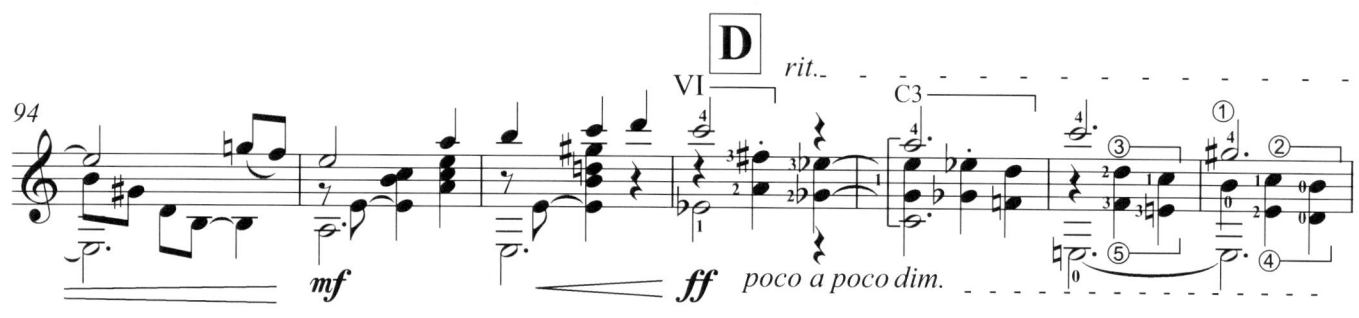

Pajarito
(Little Bird)

Michael N. Bellmont

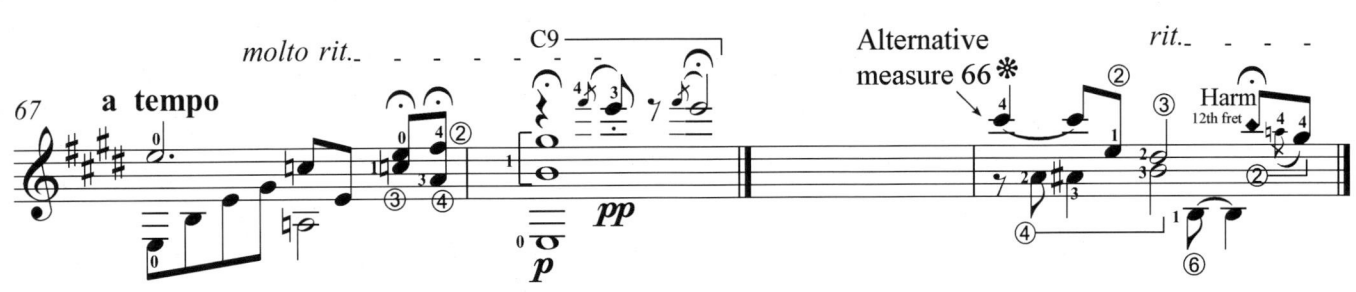

Passage

- Take liberty with the tempo.
- Allow all notes to ring wherever possible for a harp-like effect.

Michael N. Bellmont

𝅗𝅥=52

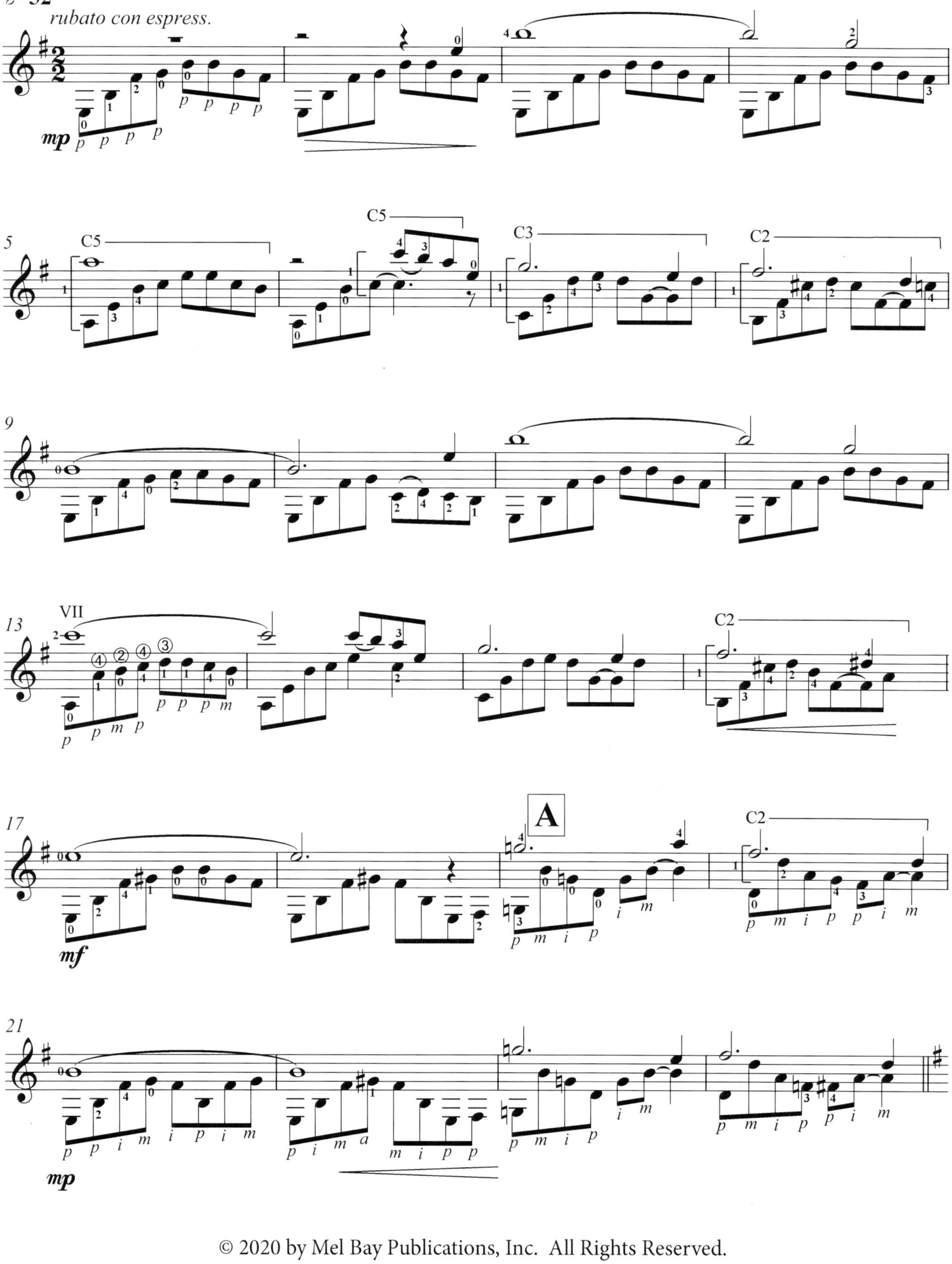

rubato con espress.

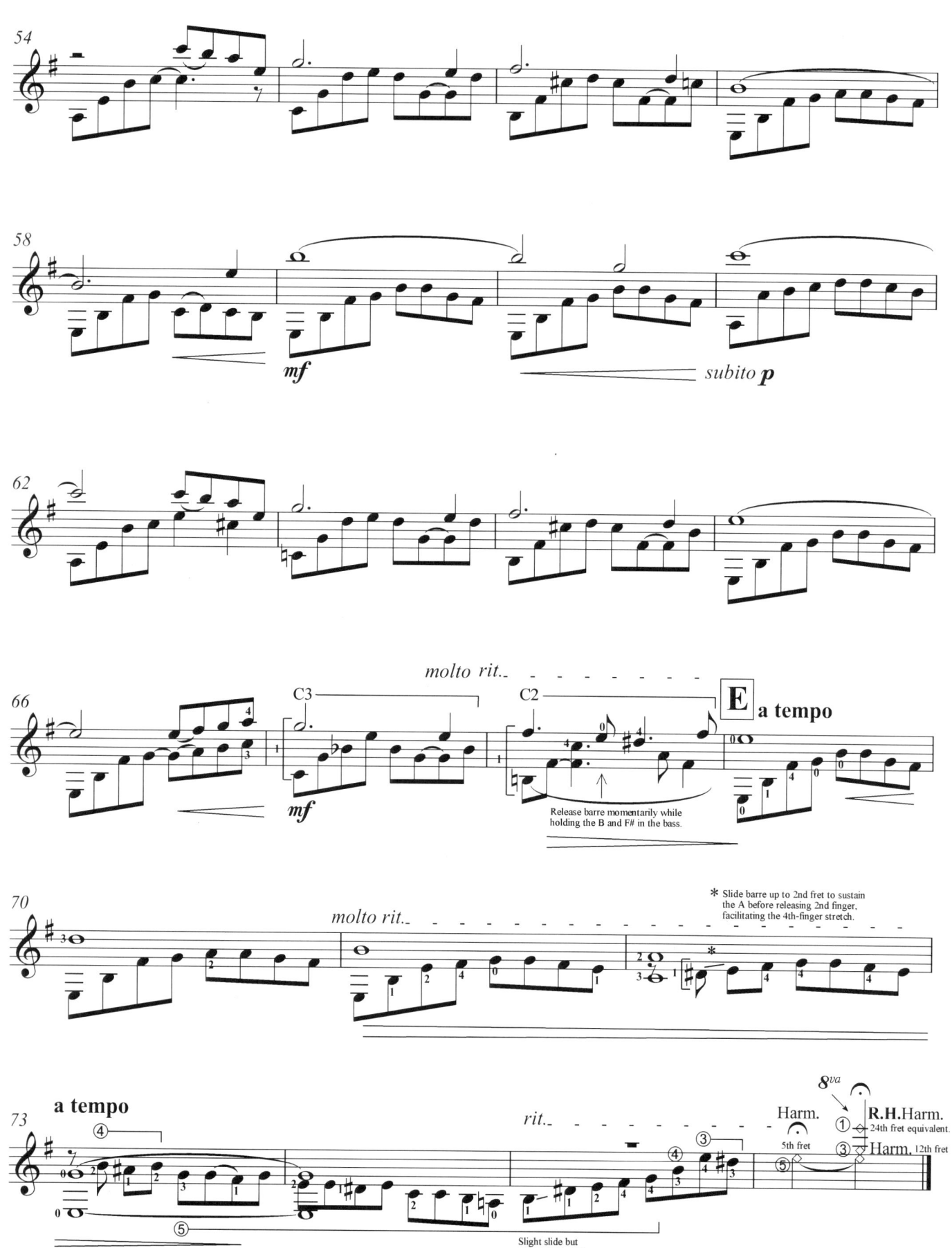

Rain/After the Rain

Michael N. Bellmont

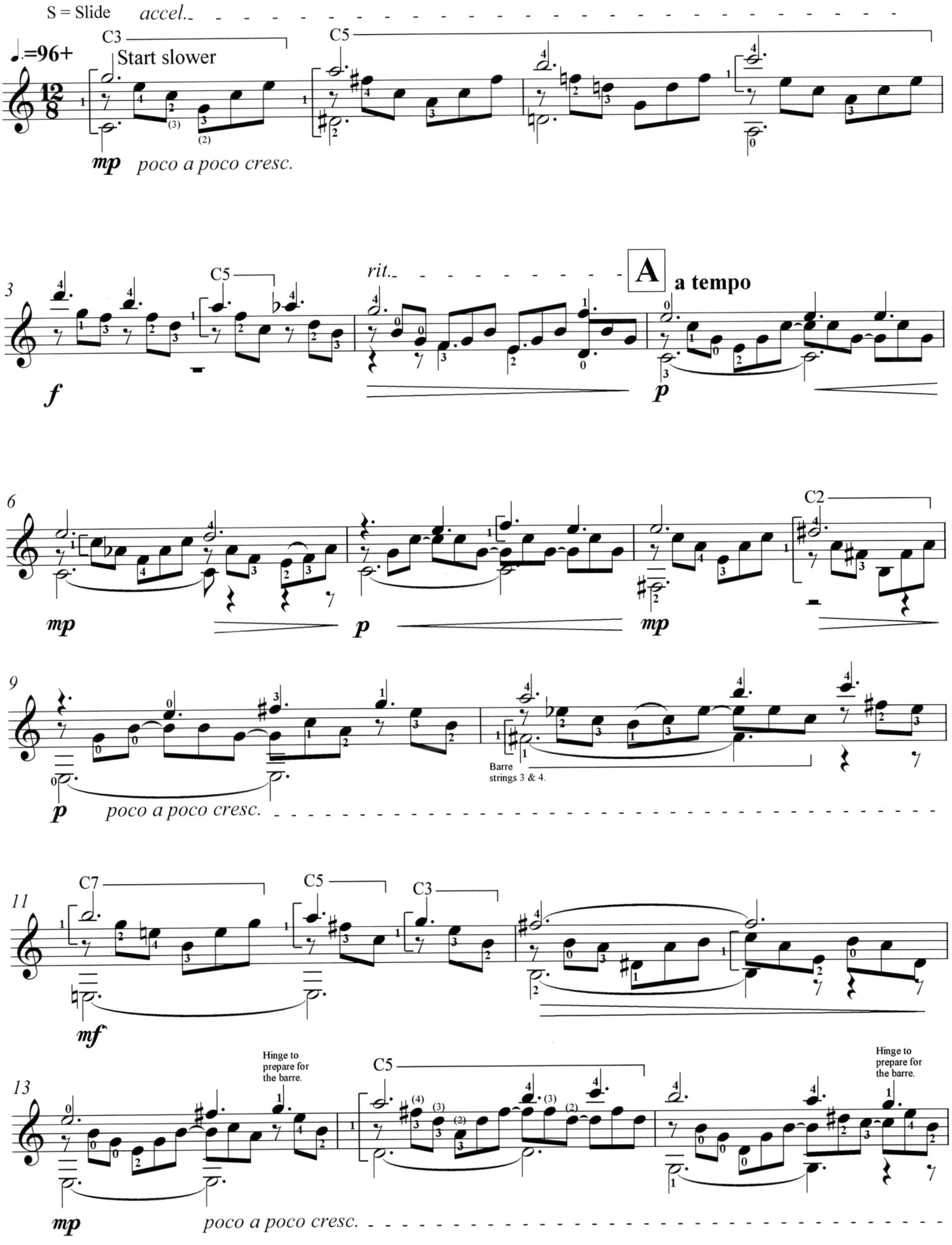

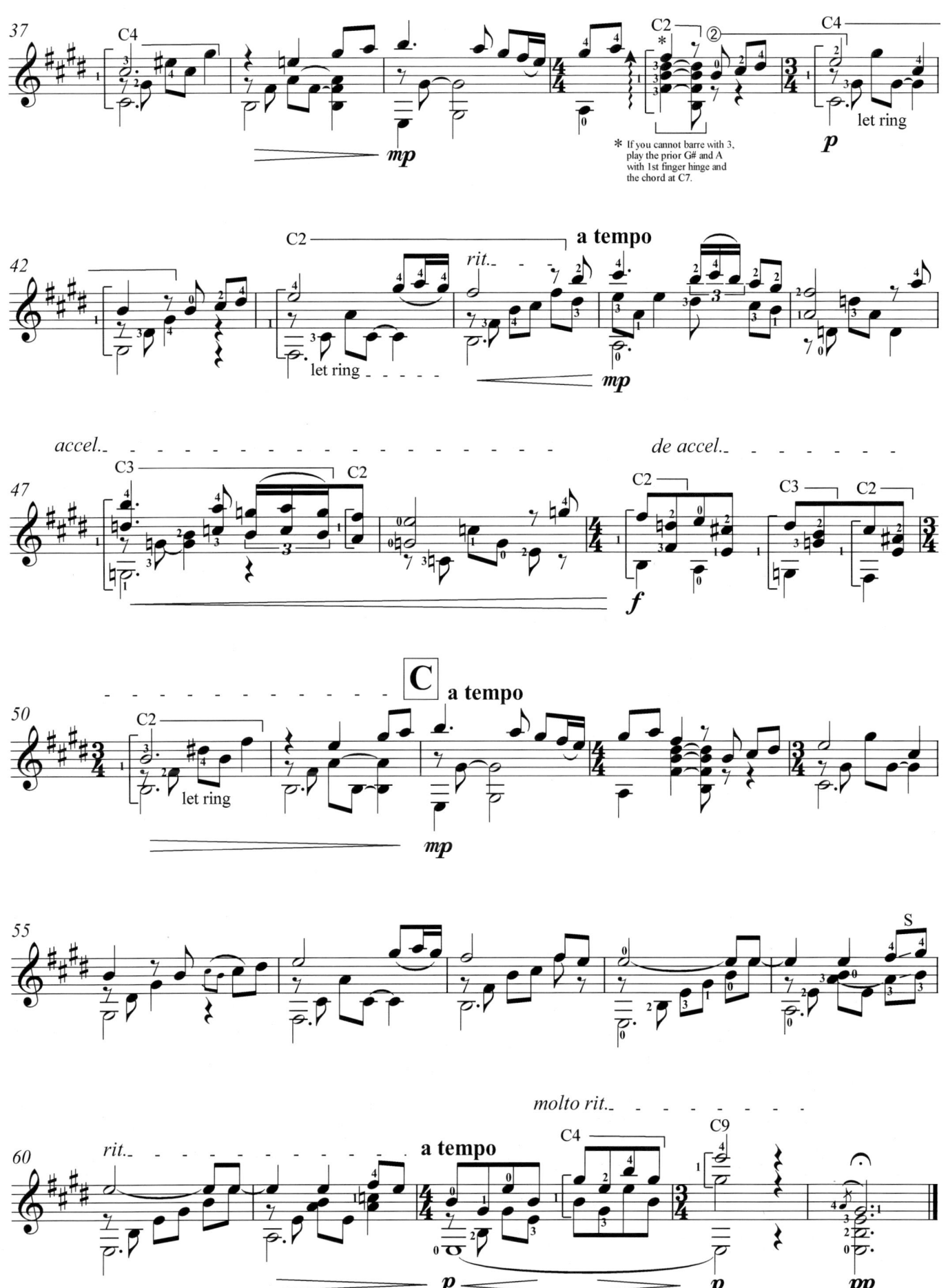

Something Samba

Michael N. Bellmont

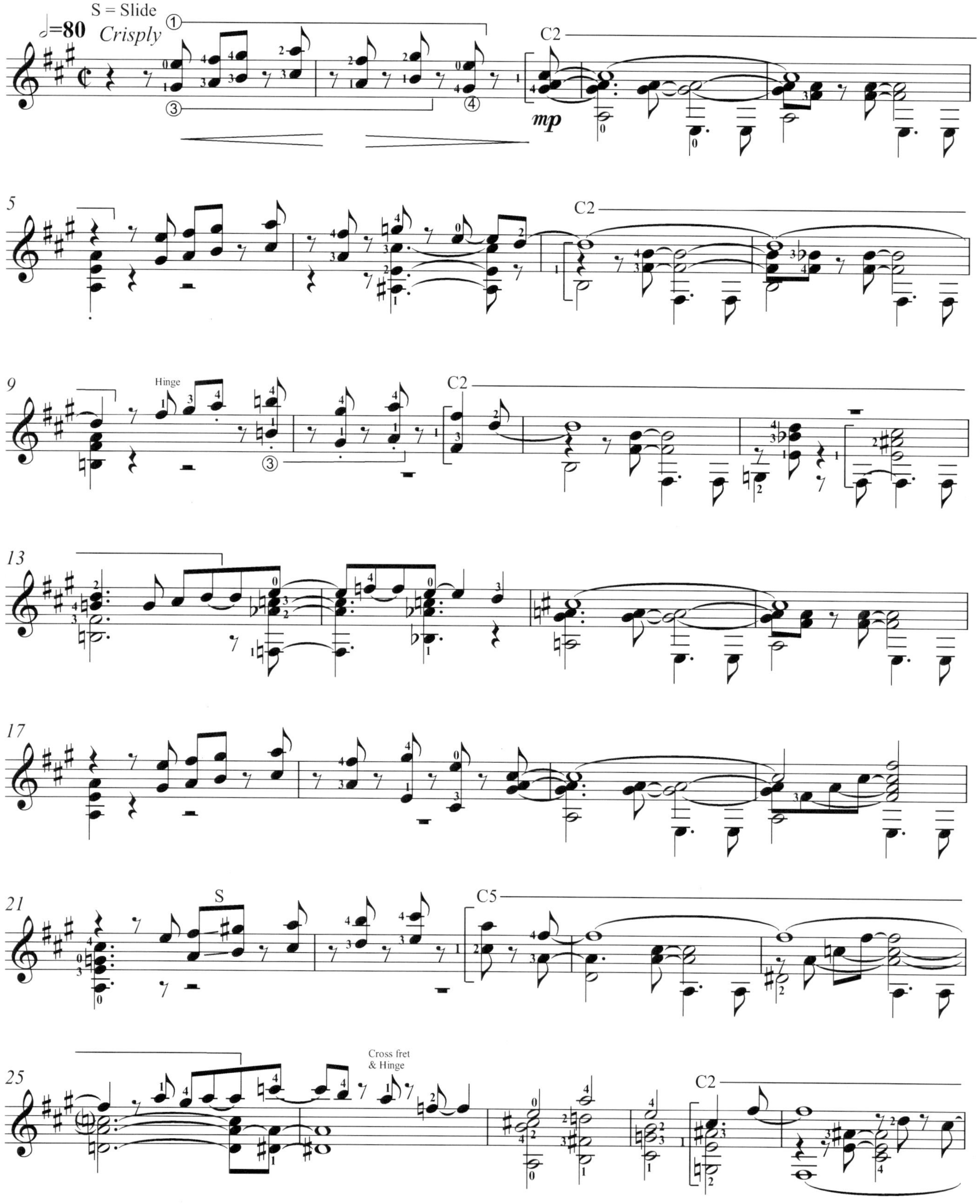

Soñadora

Michael N. Bellmont

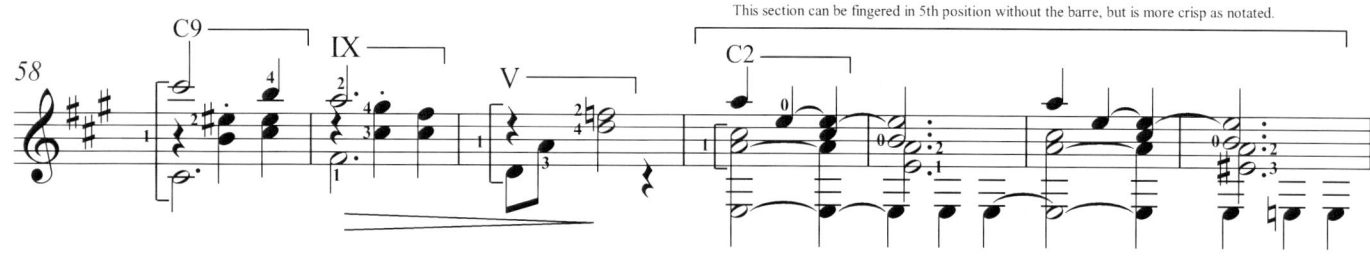

Sueño Español

Michael N. Bellmont

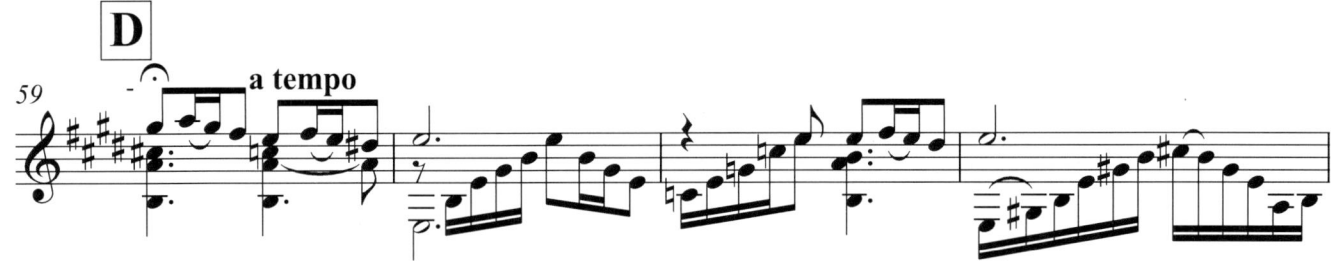
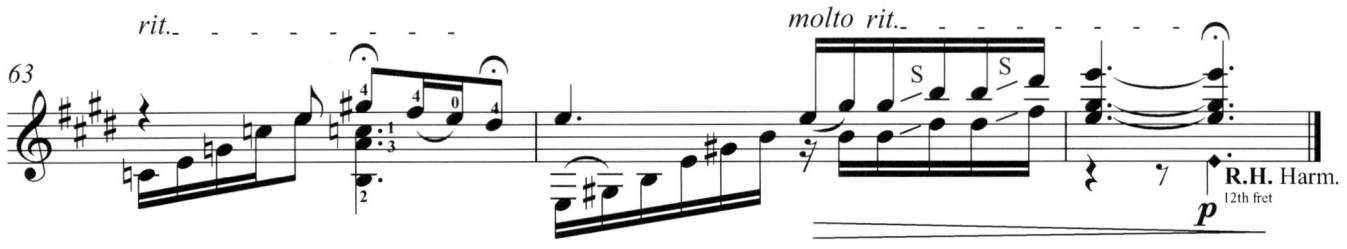

Tango Cromático

♩= 90+ *(Smokin')*
♩=84 *(Ideal)*
♩=74 *(Not too shabby)*
♩=64 *(Gettin' there)*

Michael N. Bellmont

rubato with intensity

© 2020 by Mel Bay Publications, Inc. All Rights Reserved.

Tango Español

Michael N. Bellmont

S = Slide

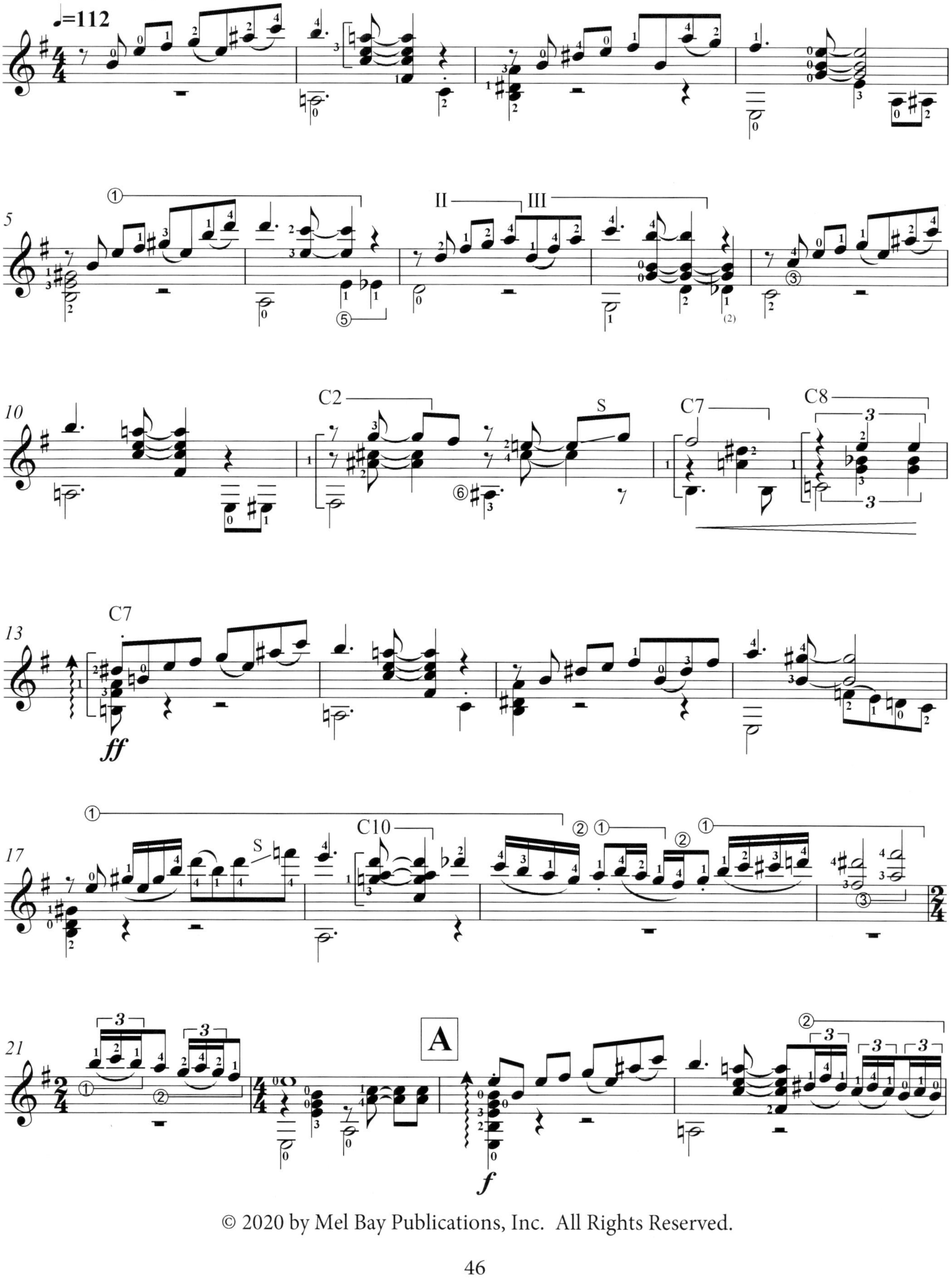

With energy and movement

Tango Loco

Michael N. Bellmont

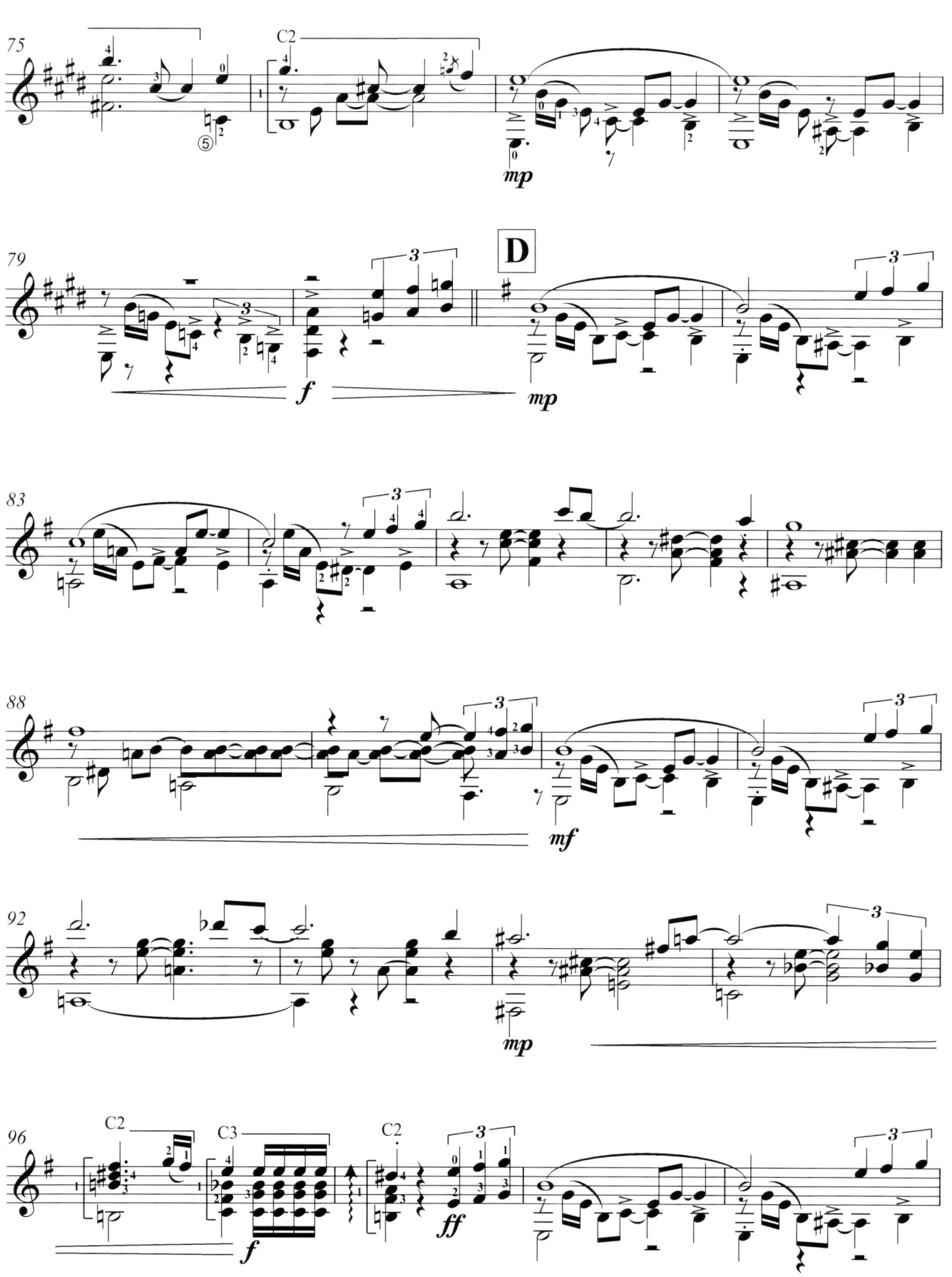

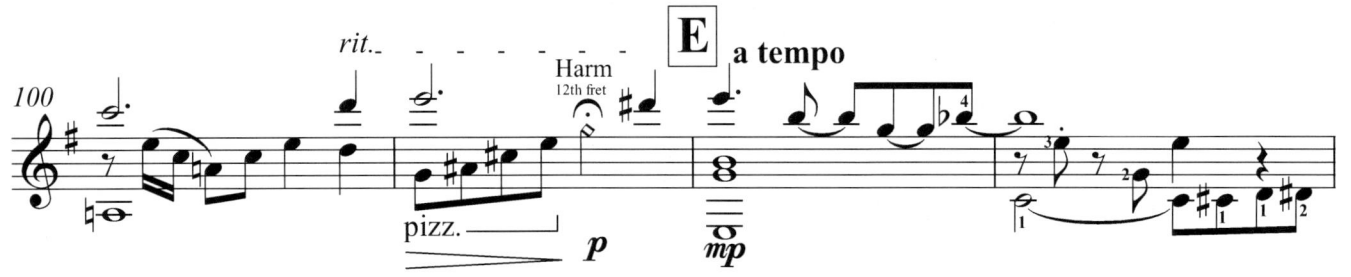

Tango para Guillermo
(Tango for William)

Michael N. Bellmont

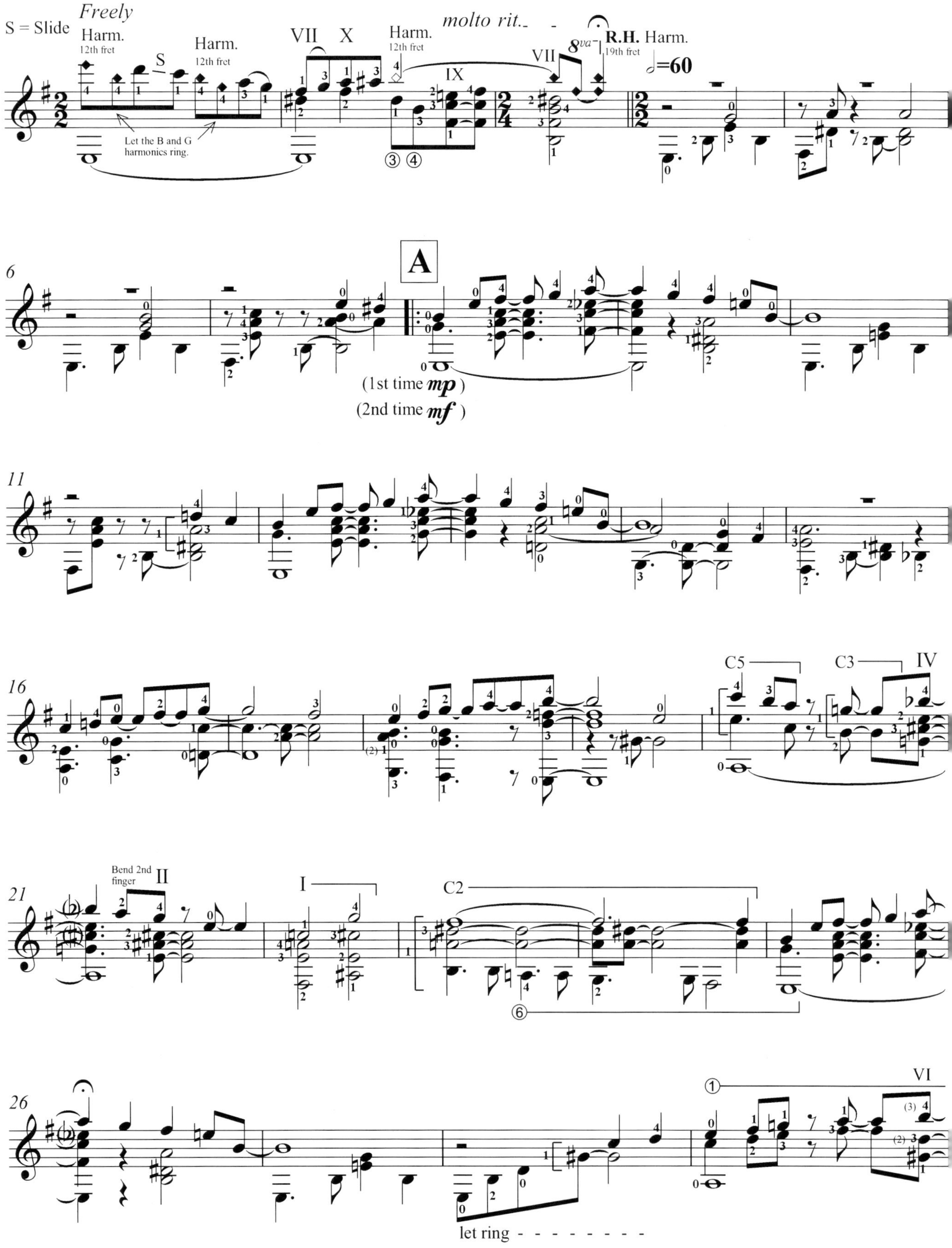

Texas Tango

Michael N. Bellmont

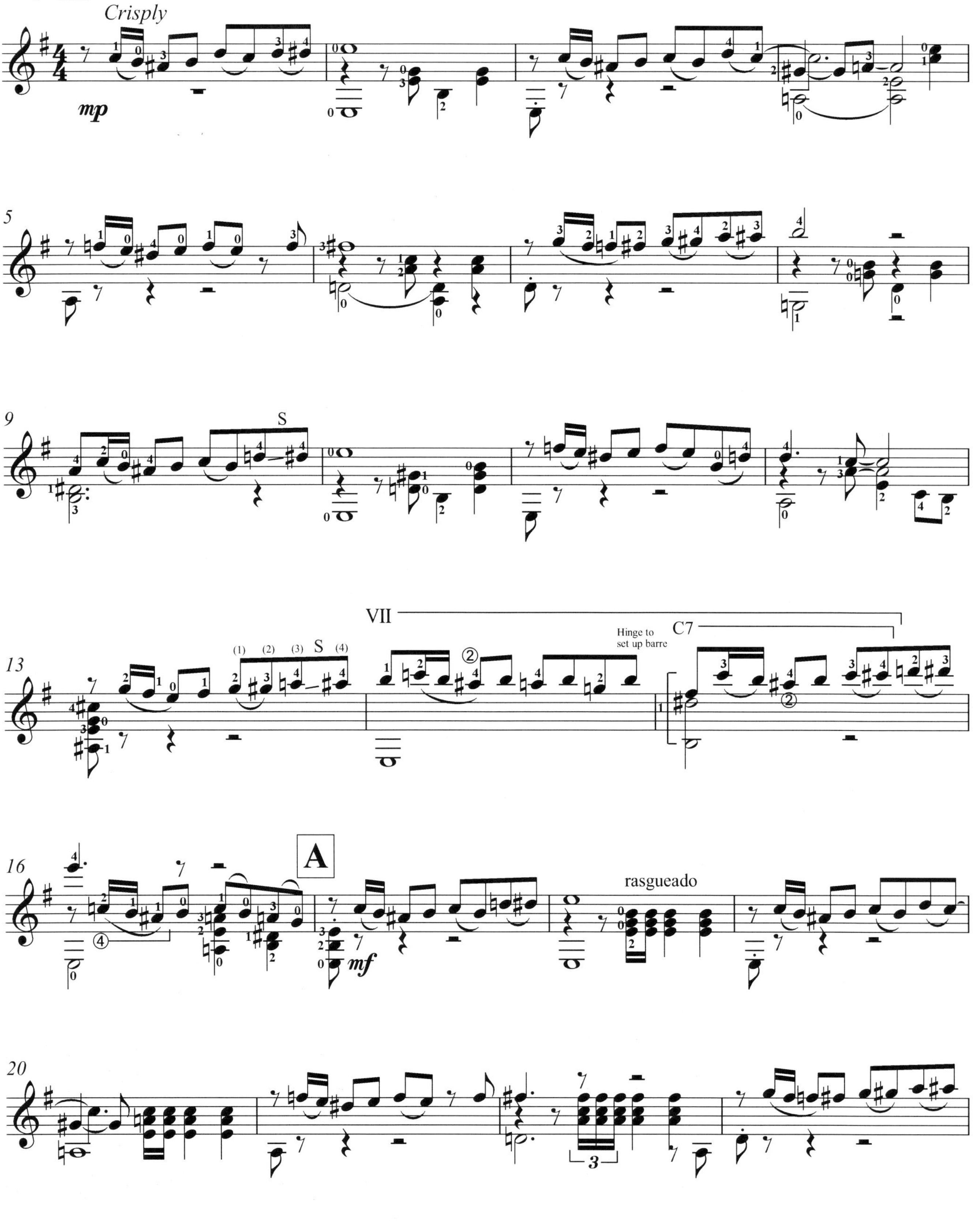

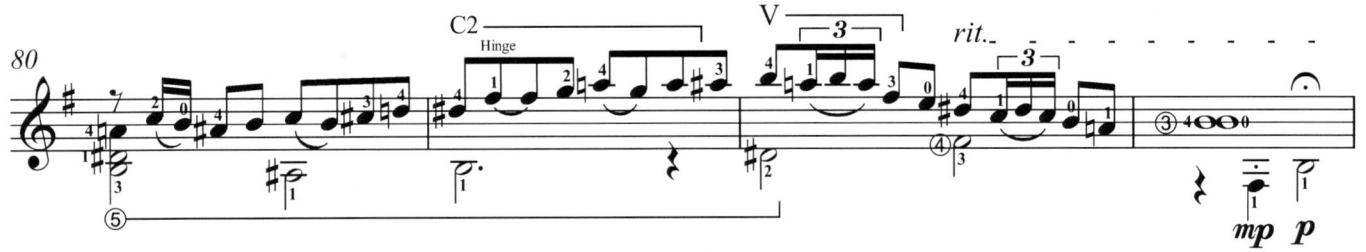

About the Author

Michael Bellmont

Raised in Houston, Texas, Michael Bellmont grew up surrounded by a broad range of musical styl from blues, rock, and Latin, to gospel, Dixieland, and jazz standards. That background, coupled with a formal music education and degree in Classical Guitar Performance, has given him a reputation for extraordinary versatility in both composing and performing. In addition to this instrumental collection he has composed well over 1,000 songs in every imaginable style, includir music and lyrics for two full-length musicals. For Michael Bellmont, there are no musical borders

Other Recommended Mel Bay Guitar Solo Books

J. S. Bach French Suite No. 5 in C Major (Ausqui)

12 Spanish Dances by Granados (Griggs)

Classical and Flamenco Guitar Solos and Etudes (E. Hochman/J. Hochman)

España: Opus 165 by Albéniz (Griggs)

Granados: Romantic and Poetic Scenes (Griggs)

Isaac Albéniz: 26 Pieces Arranged for Guitar (S. Yates)

Ernesto Cordero: Two Popular Andalusian Themes

Romance Variations (Stover)

Selected Works of Enrique Granados for Solo Guitar (Barreiro)

Spanish Composers for Classical Guitar (Afshar)

Spanish Dance No. 5: Andaluza by Enrique Granados arr. by Pepe Romero

Treasures of the Spanish Guitar (De Chiaro)

Valses Poeticos by Enrique Granados (Afshar)

Album of Pieces for Solo Guitar Volume 1 (Diego)

Antonio Carlos Jobim for Classical Guitar (Bellinati)

Classic Guitar Solos on Latin American Rhythms (Morel)

Contemporary Guitar Composers of the Americas (multiple composers)

Ernesto Cordero: El Carbonerito

Ernesto Nazareth: Brazilian Tangos (Newman)

Ernesto Nazareth: Guitar Solo Anthology (Medeiros/Almada)

Julio S. Sagreras Guitar Lessons Books 1-3

Julio S. Sagreras Guitar Lessons Books 4-6

Lullabies of the Americas (Barreiro)

Music of Jorge Morel

Selected Guitar Solos Volume 1 (Morel)

Selected Guitar Solos Volume 2 (Morel)

Selected Guitar Solos Volume 3 (Morel)

Soledad (Almeida)

Suite Antillana for Solo Guitar (Cordero)

The Complete Works of Agustin Barrios Mangoré for Guitar Vol. 1 (Stover)

The Complete Works of Agustin Barrios Mangoré for Guitar Vol. 2 (Stover)

The Magnificent Guitar of Jorge Morel: A Life of Music (McClellan/Bratic)

WWW.MELBAY.COM

Other Recommended Mel Bay Guitar Solo Books

13 Easy Brazilian Choros for Solo Guitar (Almada)

Anthology of Popular Brazilian Music of the 19th Century (Almada/Medeiros)

Brazilian Electric Guitar (Almada/Medeiros)

Brazilian Jazz Guitar (M. Christiansen/Zaradin)

Brazilian Jazz Guitar Styles (Barbosa-Lima/Griggs)

Danzas Cubanas of Ignacio Cervantes (Barreiro)

Guitar Music of Cuba (Barreiro)

Hispanic-American Guitar (Back)

Homage to Latin Music - Salsa (Morel)

Jack Jezzro: Brazilian Nights (Carlson)

Jorge Morel: Latin American Rhythms for Guitar

Latin American Guitar Ensembles (Montes)

Latin American Guitar Guide (Stover)

Latin American Jazz for Fingerstyle Guitar (Zaradin)

Latin American Songs for Guitar (Silverman)

Latinas for Two (Montes)

Latinitas for Solo Guitar (Montes)

Mariachi Favorites for Solo Guitar (Sobrino/Eckels)

Music of Latin America for Acoustic Guitar (Barreiro)

Music of Mexico for Acoustic Guitar Volume 1 (Delgado)

New Wave Latin Guitar (Zaradin)

Popular Guitar Styles: Latin & Salsa (Wolters)

Popular Guitar Styles: Reggae & Music of the Islands (Wolters)

Popular Guitar Styles: Samba & Bossa Nova (Wolters)

Tangos & Milongas for Solo Guitar (Morel)

Tangos & Milongas for Solo Guitar Volume 2 (Morel)

The Complete Laurindo Almeida Anthology of Latin American Guitar Duets

Definitive de Falla (Ausqui)

WWW.MELBAY.COM